Boffin .Club

GREAT FIRE OF LONDON

MARK ALBERT SMITH · FELIPE FRANCO MATTHEW

NEON10

www.neon10.com
www.boffin.club

First published in 2017 by NEON10 Limited

Concept and Design by Mark Albert Smith
Illustrations by Felipe Franco Matthew
Contributions by Esther Galiano

ISBN 979 8 6486 0405 6

NEON10

First Floor, Telecom House
125-135 Preston Road
Brighton
East Sussex
BN1 6AF
United Kingdom

www.neon10.com
www.boffin.club

A special thanks to Maya, Arthur and Robert

CONTENTS

1One Night at the Theatre

SATURDAY SEPTEMBER 1ST 1666

My wife and I to the theatre and the play being done, we to Islington, and there eat and drank and mighty merry; and so home singing, and, after a letter or two at the office, to bed. My maid Jane called us up about three in the morning, to tell us of a great fire they saw in the City. So I rose and slipped on my nightgowne, and went to her window, but, being unused to such fires, I thought it far enough off; and so went to bed again and to sleep.

Spot the three differences between this devil and the one on stage

SAMUEL PEPYS (Aged 33 in 1666)

Pepys (pronounced PEEPS) was born nearly 400 years ago in London. He worked for the British government, and helped make the Royal Navy better. However, he is really famous because he wrote a diary. He lived through exciting times, including the Plague, the Great Fire of London and the Civil War (when two groups in England were battling to decide who should rule). He wrote about these things, but also about his life in London, his home, his wife, and his friends.

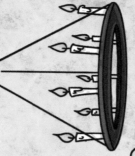

THEATRES AT WAR

The King gave his permission for there to be two London theatre companies. The King's Company and The Duke's Company. Each wanted their theatres to be the biggest and most splendid, but both had them designed by Christopher Wren, so they ended up looking quite similar!

Nell Gwynn worked at the King's theatre selling oranges, but became the most famous actress of her time, and was a great friend of the King.

Everyone loved the comedies: usually about a rich and handsome young man and a cheeky girl.

Theatres were fitted with moveable scenery and machines for thunder, lightning, and wave effects.

It was exciting to see actresses at the theatre. In Shakespeare's time women were not allowed on the stage, and so young men had to dress up to play queens, princesses and witches.

THE DEVIL

In theatre the figure of the devil was especially comedic. He would appear on the stage as a deformed and hairy sprite, with horns, dragon's wings, long tail and cloven feet, and was subjected to the greatest cruelties and indignities for the enjoyment of the audience. We pity the actor performing in that the devil costume!

2 TRUTHS, 1 LIE

You don't have to be on stage to practice your drama. There are loads of fun games you can play either at home or in the playground at school. A great one is "2 Truths, 1 Lie". For this you must have a minimum of two people. Each person takes it in turn to tell the others three facts about themselves. Two of the facts must be true, but one MUST be a lie. It is then up to the others to guess which fact is the lie. An alternative would be to play the game with two lies and one truth, and then try and guess the truth. It's great fun and a perfect way to improve your acting and imagination.

Pudding Lane on Fire

THOMAS FARYNOR (Aged 50)

In 1666 Thomas held the post of 'Conduct of the King's Bakehouse', and supplied the navy with biscuits.

The fire started because the Farynors forgot to extinguish their oven before retiring for the evening.

Farynor escaped the burning building, along with his family, by climbing out through an upstairs window. His housemaid was not so lucky and fell, becoming the fire's first victim.

SATURDAY SEPTEMBER 1ST 1666

About seven rose again to dress myself. By and by Jane comes and tells me she hears that the fire begun this morning in the King's baker's house in Pudding-lane, and that above 300 houses have been burned down to-night by the fire we saw, and that it is now burning down all Fish-street, by London Bridge.

LONDON BRIDGE
Often with a gruesome display of severed heads of traitors, impaled on pikes, then dipped in tar and boiled for preservation.

The buildings were a major fire hazard.

There were over 200 buildings on the bridge. Some were 7 storeys high and overhung the road to form a dark tunnel through which all traffic had to pass.

When the bridge was busy, crossing it could take over an hour. It was London's only bridge, and so there was little choice.

MEDIEVAL FINE CAKES

A popular treat of the time. Fine Cakes are made from five easily found ingredients. More like a biscuit than a cake, they are extremely DELICIOUS. Especially if you are lucky enough to have honey to pour on top!

They are very easy to make.
Why don't you give them a try?

Ingredients
250g of Soft butter
100g of Granulated Sugar
A Flat Teaspoon of Cinnamon
240g Flour (unbleached or white)
A Pinch of Salt

Recipe (makes 9 square cakes)
Mix together the sugar, salt, flour, butter, and cinnamon. Add water as need to make the dough easier to mold and shape. Place the dough into a medium sized baking tray which has been lined with baking paper. Flatten the dough into a sheet and prick with a fork all over. Bake at 220° for 30 minutes or longer until done. Cut into squares while warm.

Thomas Farynor's biscuits were made by baking bread twice, leaving it crispy, flaky, and easy to store. They lasted a lot longer than bread which made them ideal for long journeys, such those made by the navy.

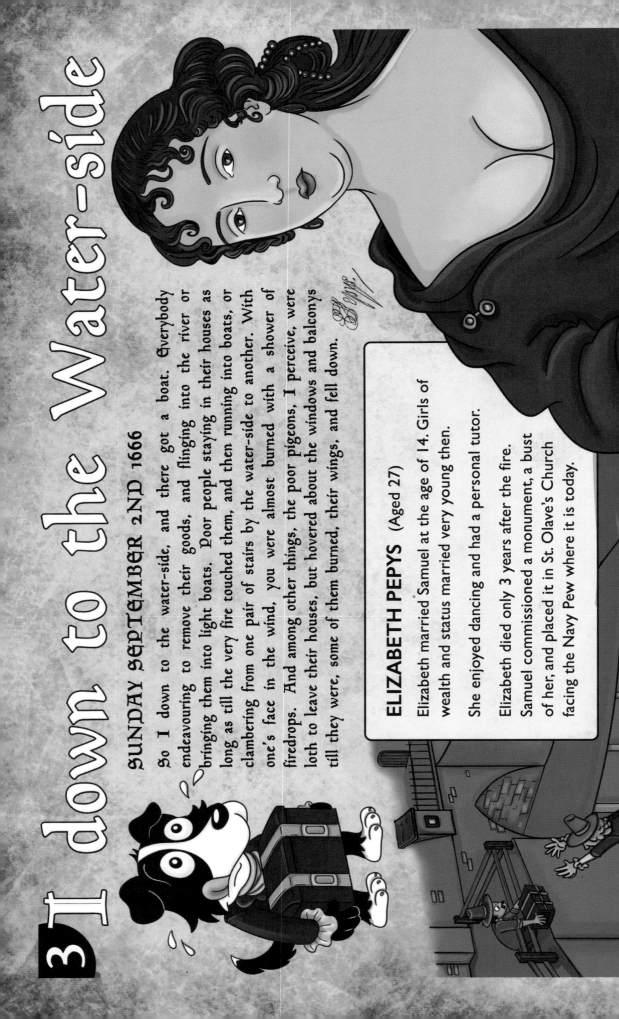

3 I down to the Water-side

SUNDAY SEPTEMBER 2ND 1666

So I down to the water-side, and there got a boat. Everybody endeavouring to remove their goods, and flinging into the river or bringing them into light boats. Poor people staying in their houses as long as till the very fire touched them, and then running into boats, or clambering from one pair of stairs by the water-side to another. With one's face in the wind, you were almost burned with a shower of firedrops. And among other things, the poor pigeons, I perceive, were loth to leave their houses, but hovered about the windows and balconys till they were, some of them burned, their wings, and fell down.

ELIZABETH PEPYS (Aged 27)

Elizabeth married Samuel at the age of 14. Girls of wealth and status married very young then.

She enjoyed dancing and had a personal tutor.

Elizabeth died only 3 years after the fire. Samuel commissioned a monument, a bust of her, and placed it in St. Olave's Church facing the Navy Pew where it is today.

THE RIVER THAMES

There was only one bridge over the River Thames, so boats were very important for carrying people and goods. The fire could not spread across the river, so people escaped by boat to the south side where they knew they would be safe.

The poorer districts along the riverfront had stores and cellars of combustibles, which are things that easily catch fire. Along the wharves, the rickety wooden tenements (flats) and warehouses held tar, pitch, hemp, and flax. All set to burst into flames and help the fire spread.

There had been a drought in 1666 and the water level in the Thames was very low. This was one of the reasons it took so long to put out the fire.

Cities usually grow up around a river as this was the best way to transport building materials, such as stone, bricks and timber (wood) before the invention of railways and vehicles such as lorries, trains and planes.

Down by the river there were also muskets (guns) and gunpowder, left over from the civil war between the old King and Oliver Cromwell's Model Army; all ready to explode!

ST PAUL'S CHURCH

The first St Paul's Church on this site was built in 604 – it burnt down 71 years later. It's replacement was destroyed by Viking raiders in 962.

The St Paul's that burnt down in 1666 was actually the 5th church built.

The fire was so hot that heat from it melted the lead roof on the church. The lead was then seen flowing down the nearby streets.

St Paul was an important saint because he was one of the disciples of Jesus. He wrote about Christ's life, and is the patron saint of authors.

After the fire a new cathedral was designed by Sir Christopher Wren

THE TOWER OF LONDON

William the Conqueror ordered the Tower of London to be built in 1066.

Originally a safe home for the new King, it has also been used as a prison, a place to keep the crown jewels and as a menagerie, which is a zoo for unusual animals. The tower housed elephants, tigers, kangaroos and ostriches.

The reason the Tower didn't catch fire was thought to be because of the 'glacis', an open sloping area around the White Tower built for defence.

In fact it was just as well it didn't catch fire, as there were over 500 tons of gunpowder stored in its cellars left over from the Civil War. BOOM!

An Audience with the King

SUNDAY SEPTEMBER 2ND 1666

having staid, and in an hour's time seen the fire: rage every way, and nobody, to my sight, endeavouring to quench it, but to remove their goods, and leave all to the fire, and the wind mighty high and driving it into the City. I to White hall to the Kings closet. I did tell the King and Duke of Yorke what I saw, and that unless his Majesty did command houses to be pulled down nothing could stop the fire. The King commanded me to go to my Lord Mayor and command him to spare no houses, but to pull down before the fire every way.

KING CHARLES II (Aged 36)

Charles was known by his friends as the Merry Monarch because he kept a happy court.

He declared the fire an act of God.

He helped organise the fire-fighting, and even joined his brother James, to throw water on the flames.

He sailed down from Whitehall in the royal barge to inspect the scene and found that things were not good in spite of Mayor Bloodworth's assurances.

After the fire he appointed Christopher Wren as the lead architect, and saw all of London rebuilt.

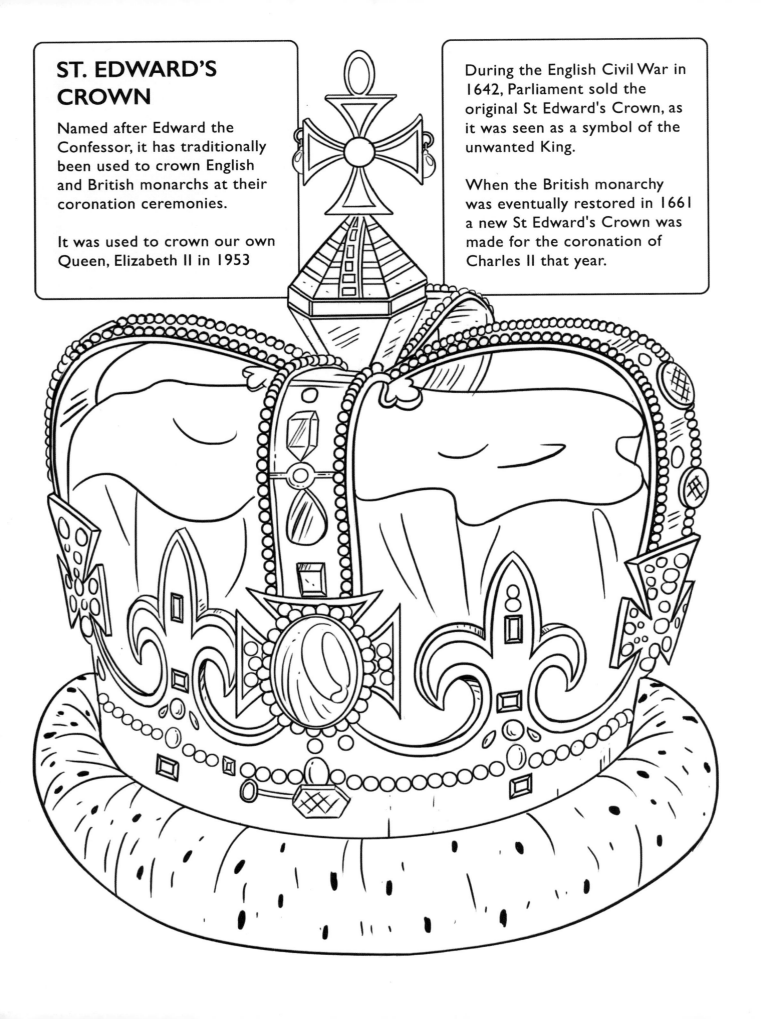

ST. EDWARD'S CROWN

Named after Edward the Confessor, it has traditionally been used to crown English and British monarchs at their coronation ceremonies.

It was used to crown our own Queen, Elizabeth II in 1953

During the English Civil War in 1642, Parliament sold the original St Edward's Crown, as it was seen as a symbol of the unwanted King.

When the British monarchy was eventually restored in 1661 a new St Edward's Crown was made for the coronation of Charles II that year.

KING'S COURTIERS

The King always expected his more important nobles to spend much of the year in attendance with him at court.

This also included clergy, soldiers, clerks, secretaries, and ambitious business men.

King Charles II court was very joyful, with song, dance, and the best food available.

On his deathbed Charles apologised to his courtiers, "I am sorry, gentlemen, for being such a time a-dying." The party was over.

5 Escaping with their Lives

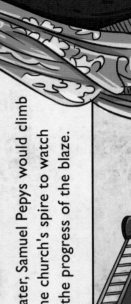

SATURDAY SEPTEMBER 1ST 1666

I walked along Watling street, as well as I could, every creature coming away loaden with goods to save, and here and there sicke people carried away in beds. Extraordinary goods carried in carts and on backs.

Then going to the fire, I find, by the great help given by the workmen out of the King's yards, sent up by Sir W Penn, there is a good stop given to it.

SIR WILLIAM PENN

William was an Admiral in the Royal Navy and was also Pepys' next door neighbour.

During the fire he rescued many important buildings by commanding his men from a nearby naval yard to demolish the surrounding buildings and create fire breaks.

One such building was "All Hallows by the Tower", an ancient church overlooking the Tower of London. Founded in 675, it is one of the oldest churches in London.

Later, Samuel Pepys would climb the church's spire to watch the progress of the blaze.

THE DAMAGE DONE

The fire was very costly for London and it's people, both rich and poor.

At least £10,000,000 (ten million) pounds of damage was done. That is £40,000,000,000 (forty billion) pounds if it were today.

15,000 homes were destroyed leaving 85% of the population homeless.

The first victim of the fire was the Farynor's maid, and there are only 5 other recorded deaths. Perhaps there are more we don't know about!

In the cold winter that followed many more died, huddled within the ruins of their homes or in makeshift communities along the riverside.

Some places smouldered for months. Many people chose to go and live elsewhere. It took almost 50 years to fully rebuild the city.

There were no hospitals. Doctors were expensive and not good, compared with those we have today.

A poultice was a common way to treat burns. Made from things such as horse manure, pig fat, rotten vegetables, fresh eggs, hen's droppings and horse urine. It actually helped a lot.

THE BLACK DEATH

The people of London were used to all sorts of dangers. The year before had seen a fresh outbreak of the the Black Death. Also known as the plague, it had already killed millions of people.

In 1665 it began slowly. By May just 43 people had died. But in June 6137 died, in July 17036 and at its peak in August, 31159 people died in what was a terrible summer.

It was caught by living in filthy conditions, next to rats and fleas.

It would begin with lumps under the armpits and red and black spots on the skin, then finally a fever would develop with the vomiting of blood.

It was difficult to treat and very contagious. Some doctors wore a beak-like mask filled with aromatic things such as dried flowers, spices, herbs, and vinegar. They thought it protected them from the disease.

Most victims died after two to seven days of falling ill.

It is thought the fire played an important part in stopping the plague's spread.

6 Pulling Down the houses

SUNDAY SEPTEMBER 2ND 1666

At last met my Lord Mayor in Canning street. To the King's message he cried, "Lord! what can I do? People will not obey me. I have been pulling down houses; but the fire overtakes us faster than we can do it." I walked home to see the churches all filling with goods.

ACT NOW!

Imagine you are the Mayor of London. Put a cross through the houses that you would demolish to create a fire break

THOMAS BLOODWORTH (Aged 46)

Lord Mayor Bloodworth at first refused to pull houses down, as it was wasteful and he was worried that he would have to personally pay the price for doing so.

Early, upon seeing the fire, he decided that it was not dangerous. He returned home and went back to sleep.

Pepys described Thomas as "a silly man, I think."

CITY OF LONDON

London was established by merchants trading on the River Thames shortly before the Roman conquest of 47 AD. The Romans called it "Londinium". It became an important port, and they built a wall around it. Parts of this wall can still be seen today.

At the time of the great fire there was still only one bridge. London Bridge was first built by the Romans 1600 years before, from wood. Today 24 bridges span the Thames. Most are roadbridges, some are for the railway, and there is even a footbridge. There are also 5 tunnels dug under the river.

The Latin motto of the City is "Domine dirige nos", which translates as "Lord, guide us". It appears to have been adopted in the 17th Century, not long before the great fire.

Can you write that motto into the emblem above? Write one word on each part of the bottom strip.

Above is how the emblem looked in 1666. It is slightly different today. It represents the City of London, which was nearly all of London in 1666.

It has dragon's wings bearing the red cross of St George, the patron saint of England. Today London is a lot larger and comprises of many boroughs which all have their own coat of arms.

Hand held water squirts were good at directing the water into the centre of the fire, but slow to refill.

The navy used gunpowder to blow up houses and create a good fire break.

Fire Hooks were used to pull down the buildings to prevent the spread of fire. It was a dangerous and difficult job.

The people formed chains with buckets made out of leather and filled with water from the Thames.

Axes were used to dig up and break open underground pipes to release the water.

Early fire engines were good at putting out small fires quickly, as they could be stored full of water and ready for use, but they were soon emptied and had to be refilled. Against a big fire they were less effective and required a lot of people to operate.

Moving them was difficult.

FIRE FIGHTERS

There was no fire brigade, so no one group was responsible for putting out the fire.

There were plenty of tools to use to help with the work. Which ones do you think we still use today?

As Merry as we Could be

SUNDAY SEPTEMBER 2ND 1666

By this time it was about twelve o'clock; and so home, and there find my guests. We were in great trouble and disturbance at this fire, not knowing what to think of it. however, we had an extraordinary good dinner, and as merry, as at this time we could be. Then we to a little ale-house on the Bankside, and there staid till it was dark almost, and saw the fire grow; and, as it grew darker, appeared more and more, and in corners and upon steeples, and between churches and houses, as far as we could see up the hill of the City. We staid till, it being darkish, we saw the fire as only one entire arch of fire from this to the other side the bridge, and in a bow up the hill for an arch of above a mile long: it made me weep to see it.

JOHN EVELYN
(Aged 45)

He lived in Deptford, to the south of the river, so his home was safe. He also wrote a diary. On this day he wrote... "I went againe to the ruines, for it was now no longer a Citty."

The spelling of some words was different then.

LONDON'S BURNING SONG

1. Lon-don's burn - ing, Lon-don's burn - ing.

2. Fetch the en - gines, fetch the en

3. Fire! Fire! Fire! Fire!

4. Pour on wa - ter, pour on wa - ter.

RULES FOR THE GREAT FIRE OF LONDON PIGEON GAME

First make your own counters to represent each player. Colour squares of paper will do. Any number of people can play. You will also need one die. Each player takes a turn in a clockwise direction. All players start away from the board. The first person to land on 63 wins the game.

BRIDGES

Each time a player lands on one of the 2 bridges they are automatically transported to the other bridge and then must take another turn.

⑥ ⇅ ⑫

DICE

Same with Dice. Move to the other dice space and take another turn.

㉖ ⇅ ㊵

PIGEONS

Each time a player lands on a Pigeon they automatically jump forward to the next Pigeon on the board. Then they IMMEDIATELY must roll the die to take another turn. NOTE. There is a Pigeon at 63, so if you land at 59 you jump to 63 and win the game.

⑤ ⑨ ⑭ ⑱ ㉓ ㉗ ㉜ 63 ㊱ ㊶ ㊺ ㊿ 54 59

MISSED TURNS

Land on either of these and you will miss a turn.

Land on either of these and you will miss 2 turns.

⑲ 52 ㉛ 42 42

DEATH

Land on Death and you go back to the beginning.

58

WINNING THE GAME

To win the game you must roll the exact number required to reach the final space, 63.

REBOUNDING

Any roll over what is needed to reach 63 results in you bouncing back the additional spaces. For instance, if you are on 60, and roll a 6. You go forward 3 then rebound 3, ending up back at 60. Rebound to 59 and win the game. Avoid Death!

The GREAT FIRE of LONDON

PIDGEON GAME

63

8People Fetch Things Away

boats
cat
diary
pidgeon
london
cheese
fire
bucket
pepys
plague
bakery
crown
pie
gunpowder

```
P P G M Z I R H D N L B D L X
I L Z M H D C R N K B U D M F
E A M Z F T F T T W O C Q S B
H G Q K M M D D Q J A K U D D
A U L N L R Z Y B W T E B T I
I E T V S B F C A T S T B A A
R Q Q E Z K X P H H Y P E K R
M Q W X Z C H E E S E C Y K Y
R G U N P O W D E R V P A W C
L H N N K M K L F U L I V M S
O M N L P B C O O P P D J H T
C R O W N F K N R P Q G L F P
P E P Y S D F D V H K E T I L
O B A K E R Y O X N W O D R X
K G U H D N E N R V D N H E K
```

THE DUKE OF YORK
(Aged 32)

James, the brother of Charles II, would eventually become King after Charles' death in 1685.

Samuel Pepys wrote that James was fond of his children and was a good father, and played with them "like an ordinary private father of a child". His daughters, Mary and Anne, both grew up to in their turns to become Queen of England.

MONDAY SEPTEMBER 3RD 1666

We were forced to begin to pack up our owne goods and carry much of them into the garden, and I did remove my money and iron chests into my cellar, and got my bags of gold into my office. About four o'clock in the morning, my Lady Batten sent me a cart to carry away all my best things, which I did riding myself in my night-gowne in the cart; and, Lord! to see how the streets and the highways are crowded with people running and riding, and getting of carts at any rate to fetch away things. There was no passing with any thing through the postern, the crowd was so great. The Duke of Yorke of this day by the office, and spoke to us, and did ride with his guard up and down the City, to keep all quiet.

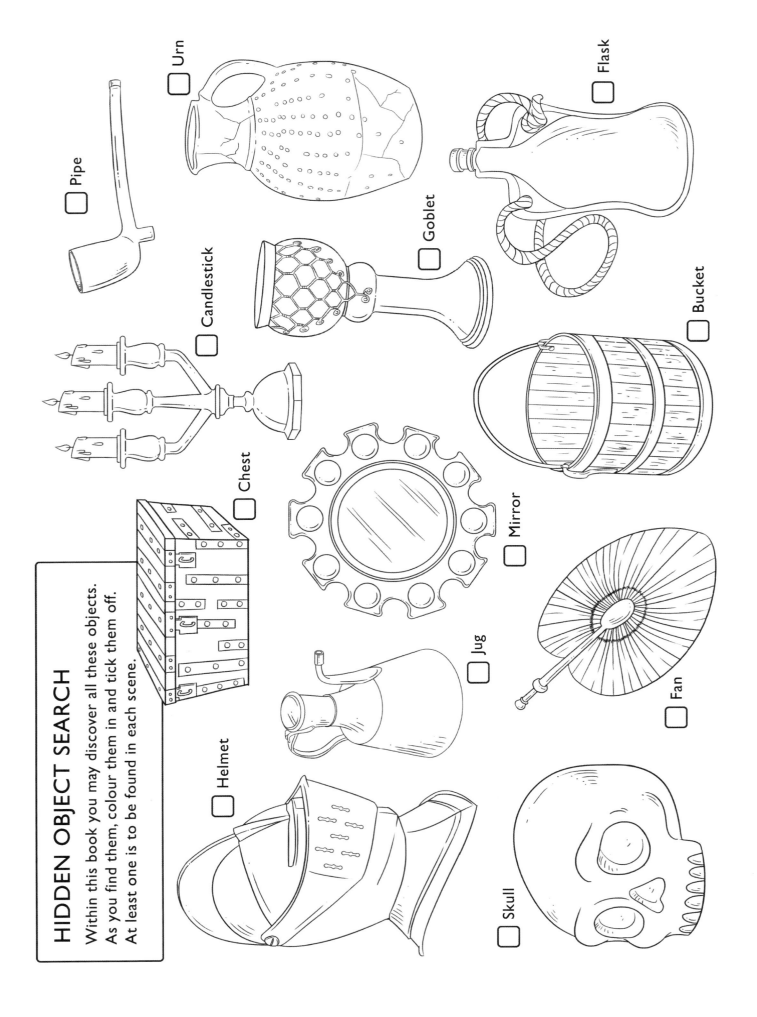

HIDDEN OBJECT SEARCH

Within this book you may discover all these objects.
As you find them, colour them in and tick them off.
At least one is to be found in each scene.

Pipe

Urn

Flask

Candlestick

Goblet

Chest

Bucket

Mirror

Jug

Helmet

Fan

Skull

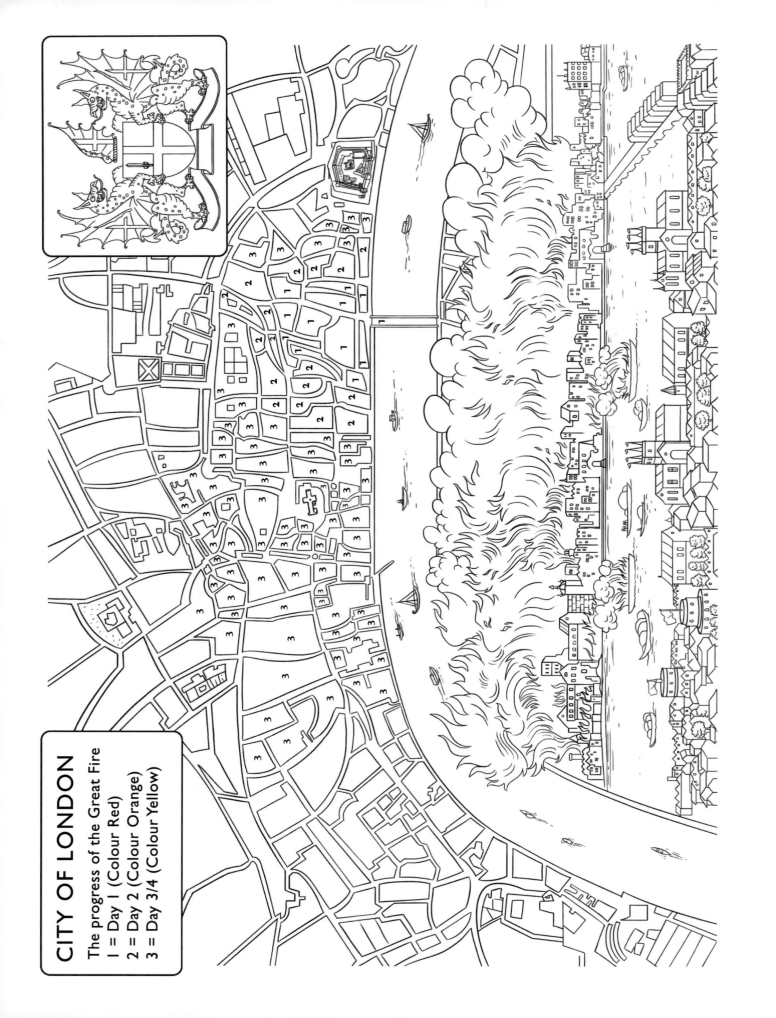

CITY OF LONDON

The progress of the Great Fire
1 = Day 1 (Colour Red)
2 = Day 2 (Colour Orange)
3 = Day 3/4 (Colour Yellow)

9 Burying the wine and cheese

TUESDAY SEPTEMBER 4Th 1666.

Up by break of day to get away the remainder of my things; Sir W. Batten not knowing how to remove his wine, did dig a pit in the garden, and laid it in there; and I took the opportunity of laying all the papers of my office that I could not otherwise dispose of. And in the evening Sir W. Penn and I did dig another, and put our wine in it; and I my Parmazan cheese, as well as my wine and some other things.

Only now and then walking into the garden, and saw how horridly the sky looks, all on a fire in the night, was enough to put us out of our wits; and, indeed, it was extremely dreadful, for it looks just as if it was at us; and the whole heaven on fire.

ROBERT HUBERT
(Aged 26)

He was a watchmaker from France.

He admitted to starting the fire by throwing a fire grenade through the window of the bakery, working with French spies and agents of the Pope.

Robert was found guilty and hanged.

However it was later proved beyond doubt that he was innocent.

He was not in London at the time, and was forced to admit to the crime during torture, so that the angry people had someone to blame.

GUESS MY TREASURE

Your house was in danger just like Samuel's. What will you save?

Make a list of objects and possessions that you would most want to quickly bury.

List only 5 items.

Then ask a friend or family member to try and guess what you have chosen.

I wonder... how well do they know you?

PEPYS' HOUSE
Seething Lane, London.

Pepys lived in a house within the Navy Office buildings on Seething Lane, just a stones throw from the Tower of London. This road no longer exisits, although there is a bust of Pepys in a small garden on the same spot today.

It was both his home and office. He earned £350/year.

He and Elizabeth both loved their home and constantly updated and renovated it. They were very happy there.

THE FASHION

In 1666 anyone who was anyone wore bright colours and ribbons.

Men wore:

Periwigs, lace and frills. Hats with feathers. High-heeled shoes. Cloaks with silk and gold braid. Small moustaches and lip-beards. Short breeches (trousers). Stockings with bunches of knee ribbons and jewelled walking sticks.

Women wore:

Full skirts with Satin petticoats. Bodices and Low cut dresses. Sleeves attached by ribbons. Or Exposed arms. Curly hair. Hats with ostrich feathers and velvet patches on faces.

THE STORY OF THE CAT

Moggy's story is not completely told. She only appears in 4 of the scenes. Can you spot her?
Complete her story by imagining where she may have been in the other 6 scenes. Then write about it or draw what happened below.

WEDNESDAY SEPTEMBER 5TH 1666.

Now begins the practice of blowing up of houses, those next the Tower, which at first did frighten people more than anything, but it stopped the fire where it was done, it bringing down the houses to the ground in the same places they stood, and then it was easy to quench what little fire was in it, though it kindled nothing almost. Walked into Moorefields (our feet ready to burn, walking through the towne among the hot coles). I did see a poor cat taken out of a hole in the chimney with the hair all burned off the body, and yet alive. But going to the fire, I find by the blowing up of houses, there is a good stop given to it. This being done to my great content, I home, and with friends supped well, and mighty merry, and our fears over.

SIR CHRISTOPHER WREN (Aged 33)

One of the most highly acclaimed English architects in history. Christopher Wren was tasked with rebuilding all the city's lost Churches.

Fifty-one parish churches were rebuilt by Christopher, however his greatest work was the design of the new St. Pauls Cathedral, especially it's dome.

With his appointment as "King's Surveyor of Works", he played an important role in designing and rebuilding London as seen today.

The fire's temperature reached 1,700 °C. This is known from tests on melted pottery fragments found recently.

That is hot enough to melt stone.

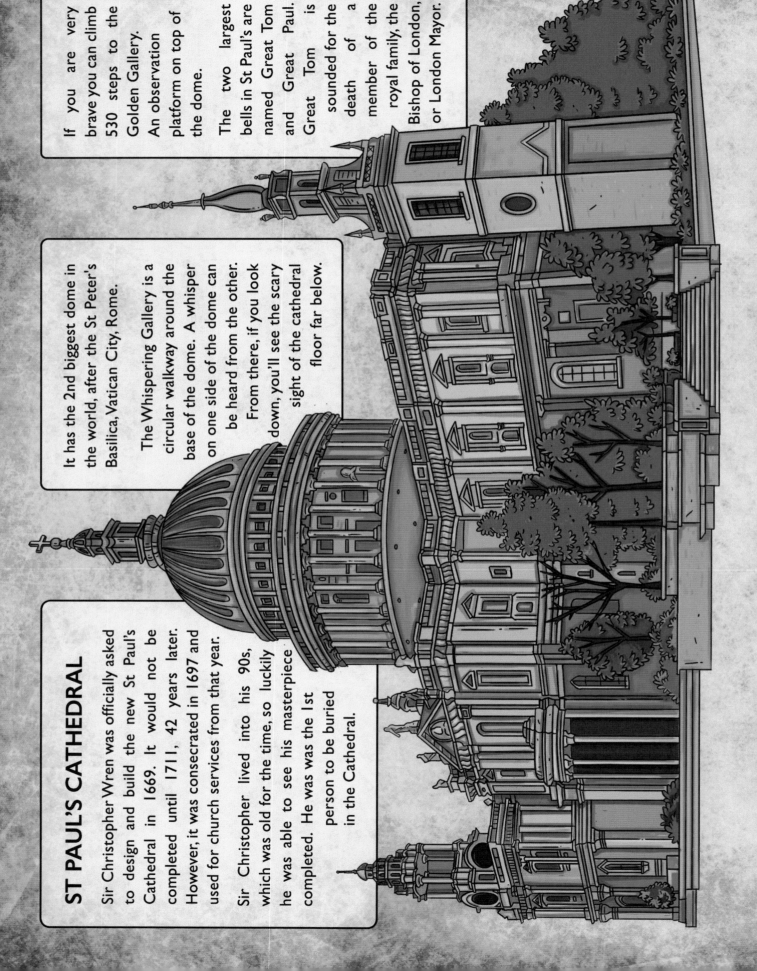

ST PAUL'S CATHEDRAL

Sir Christopher Wren was officially asked to design and build the new St Paul's Cathedral in 1669. It would not be completed until 1711, 42 years later. However, it was consecrated in 1697 and used for church services from that year.

Sir Christopher lived into his 90s, which was old for the time, so luckily he was able to see his masterpiece completed. He was was the 1st person to be buried in the Cathedral.

It has the 2nd biggest dome in the world, after the St Peter's Basilica, Vatican City, Rome.

The Whispering Gallery is a circular walkway around the base of the dome. A whisper on one side of the dome can be heard from the other. From there, if you look down, you'll see the scary sight of the cathedral floor far below.

If you are very brave you can climb 530 steps to the Golden Gallery. An observation platform on top of the dome.

The two largest bells in St Paul's are named Great Tom and Great Paul. Great Tom is sounded for the death of a member of the royal family, the Bishop of London, or London Mayor.

THE GREAT FIRE TOUR

Use Google Streetmap to experience the tour from home, just visit www.google.com/maps

① Start Here at "London Bridge". There are no houses on it these days.

② Then go to see the Church of "St Magnus the Martyr on Lower Thames Street" Rebuilt by Sir Christopher Wren.

③
PUDDING LANE EC3

④ Then Visit the "Monument to the Great Fire of London". It is 202ft high and exactly 202ft from where the fire started in Pudding Lane. Look up and you will see a flaming gilded urn, which symbolises the fire itself.

⑤ Then to "Leadenhall Market" the strong construction of the market proved an effective firebreak, and contained the fire in that direction.

⑥ Take a look at Guildhall the centre of city government since the middle ages. It survived the fire due to it's stone construction.

Also don't miss ....

"St Mary-le-Bow"

"St Paul's Cathedral"

The "Golden Boy at Pie Corner" Which was where the fire stopped.

BOFFIN CLUB
ANCIENT EGYPT

Another brainy new module from the Boffins

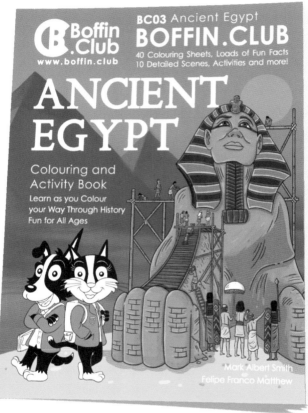

AVAILABLE IN 2022

NEON10

www.neon10.com
www.boffin.club

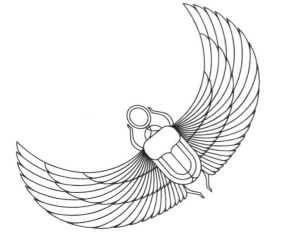

Printed in Great Britain
by Amazon